MY AI CAREER COACH

~~~~~~~~

Rob Testa

Table of Contents

***

ONE

EMBRACING AI AS YOUR PERSONAL CAREER COACH

~~~~~~~

Welcome to an exciting journey where we will explore how ChatGPT can become your very own career coach. In today's dynamic and competitive job market, having a resource that can provide guidance, support, and knowledge is invaluable. That's where ChatGPT comes in—a powerful AI tool designed to help you navigate the challenges of career development and unlock your true potential.

Before we dive into the wealth of information that awaits you in this book, let's first take a moment to discuss what ChatGPT is and how you can get set up with it. ChatGPT, or Chat-based Generative Pre-trained Transformer, is an advanced language model developed by OpenAI. It's designed to understand and generate human-like text, making it an ideal assistant for various tasks, including career development.

How do I get ChatGPT?

Getting started with ChatGPT is a breeze! Simply visit the OpenAI website (**https://openai.com/blog/chatgpt**) or utilize one of the many platforms that enable ChatGPT integration to gain access to this user-friendly AI helper. To begin, create an account on the OpenAI website, and then explore the API, following the guidelines on how to integrate ChatGPT into your preferred platform. Designed with ease of use in mind, ChatGPT caters to users of all skill levels and backgrounds. Even if you're not a tech whiz, there are plenty of tutorials and resources available to guide you through the process. In no time, you'll have your very own AI career coach at your fingertips, ready to assist you on your professional journey and make your experience simple, engaging, and rewarding, whether you're seeking help or exploring new ideas.

What are Prompts?

At its core, ChatGPT relies on a concept called "prompts" to understand and engage in real-time conversations with users. Prompts are essentially the questions or statements you input into the AI, which serve as the basis for its responses. For instance, if you need advice on choosing a theme for your wedding, you could input a prompt like *"Suggest a unique wedding theme for a beach wedding."* ChatGPT would then analyze the prompt and provide you with relevant and creative ideas based on the context.

To use ChatGPT effectively, it's essential to craft clear and specific prompts. The more precise your prompt, the more accurate and tailored the AI's response will be. If you need to refine or narrow down the AI's suggestions, you can always follow up with additional prompts to guide the conversation further. By engaging in real-time conversations with ChatGPT, you can easily and quickly obtain the answers and insights you're seeking.

***

Now that you have a better understanding of ChatGPT and how to set it up, let's take a closer look at what you can expect to find within the pages of this book. Our journey together will be divided into several chapters, each focusing on a crucial aspect of career development. We'll begin by exploring how ChatGPT can help you discover your passion, strengths, and goals to identify your ideal career path. In this section, you'll learn how to assess your skills and utilize the AI's insights to uncover new opportunities.

Next, we'll delve into the importance of building a strong professional brand, with ChatGPT as your trusted companion. You'll learn how to create an impressive resume and cover letter, develop an impactful LinkedIn profile, and navigate the world of online networking. ChatGPT's guidance will be invaluable in crafting a compelling professional persona that stands out in the competitive job market.

As we move forward, we'll focus on mastering the art of job searching. Harnessing ChatGPT's power, you'll learn how to find job openings, organize your search, and stay motivated throughout the process. With ChatGPT's assistance, you'll be better equipped to land your dream job.

Of course, no job search is complete without acing the interview process. ChatGPT will be your guide in preparing for interviews, tackling various interview questions, and making a lasting impression on potential employers. With ChatGPT's help, you'll approach interviews with confidence and poise.

Professional development and skill-building are essential aspects of a successful career, and that's where ChatGPT can once again prove invaluable. You'll discover how to use the AI to find resources for continuous learning, identify opportunities for growth, and stay competitive in your industry.

Career transitions are often challenging, but ChatGPT will be by your side, helping you manage change, identify transferable skills, and handle the emotional aspects of transition. You'll learn how to leverage your network and adapt to new professional landscapes with confidence.

Finally, we'll discuss how to climb the corporate ladder with ChatGPT as your guide. From researching opportunities to negotiating promotions and balancing your work-life commitments, ChatGPT will be an indispensable ally in your pursuit of professional success.

As we embark on this incredible adventure together, you'll not only learn the many ways ChatGPT can assist you in your professional journey but also gain a deeper understanding of how to leverage technology to your advantage. With ChatGPT as your personal career coach, you'll be better prepared to face the challenges of the ever-changing job market and achieve your career aspirations.

My aim is to empower you to take charge of your career, armed with the knowledge and support of this current AI tool. Let's start this transformative journey!

TWO

DISCOVERING YOUR PASSION & POTENTIAL

~~~~~~

Embarking on a fulfilling and successful career starts with understanding your passions, strengths, and goals. In this chapter, we'll explore how ChatGPT can help you gain a deeper understanding of yourself and identify the best career path for your unique talents and interests. Using AI tools as your career coach, you'll be able to craft a professional journey that aligns with your passions and aspirations.

Exploring Personal Interests, Strengths, and Career Goals

To begin, let's discuss how to use ChatGPT to conduct self-assessments and explore your personal interests, strengths, and career goals. Engaging in thoughtful conversations with the AI can uncover insights about your values, preferences, and aspirations. By exploring different facets of your personality and professional inclinations, you'll develop a comprehensive understanding of your interests, strengths, and goals. We will touch base on each topic and include example prompts to help jumpstart your exploration.

***

ChatGPT can help you identify your core values by asking you a series of questions about your personal beliefs, priorities, and ethics. By understanding these values, you can better align them with potential career interests. For example, if you value social justice and helping others, ChatGPT might suggest careers in social work, education, or nonprofit organizations.

Prompt: "What are my core values, and how do they align with my career interests?"

By recognizing your strengths, ChatGPT can help you understand how to leverage them effectively in your career. You may find that your top strengths are in problem-solving, creativity, or leadership. ChatGPT can suggest ways to apply these strengths in various professional settings, helping you excel in your chosen field. Additionally, ChatGPT can provide insights on how to further develop these strengths or even combine them to create unique skillsets that make you stand out in the job market.

Prompt : "What are my top strengths and how can I apply them to a professional setting?"

ChatGPT can guide you in setting realistic and achievable career goals that resonate with your personal interests and values. It can also help you identify intermediate milestones that can serve as stepping stones towards your ultimate goals. For example, if you value innovation and have an interest in technology, ChatGPT might suggest a long-term goal of becoming a tech entrepreneur or a leader in a cutting-edge industry. Intermediate milestones could include gaining experience in a specific field, obtaining relevant certifications, or building a professional network in the industry.

Prompt: "What are some long-term career goals that align with my interests and values?"

ChatGPT can analyze your interests and hobbies to reveal potential career paths that align with your passions. For instance, if you enjoy photography and visual arts, ChatGPT may suggest exploring careers in graphic design, marketing, or film production. By considering your interests, you can find a career that not only fulfills your professional goals but also brings personal satisfaction.

Prompt: "What are my main interests and hobbies, and how can they inform my career choices?"

Understanding your preferred work environment and company culture is essential for long-term career satisfaction. ChatGPT can help you evaluate your work style preferences, such as whether you prefer remote work or an office setting, a collaborative or independent work style, or a flexible or structured schedule. It can also help you identify the type of company culture that aligns with your values, such as innovation-driven, socially responsible, or employee-focused organizations.

Prompt: "What kind of work environment and company culture do I thrive in?"

By answering these prompts, you'll be able to get a comprehensive understanding of your interests, strengths, and goals, laying the foundation for a fulfilling and successful professional journey.

Assessing Your Skills and Identifying Areas for Growth

In this section, we'll dive deeper into how ChatGPT can help you assess your current skill set and identify areas for growth. This personalized feedback will help you create a roadmap for professional growth and success.

To thoroughly assess your skills and identify areas for improvement, consider using the following prompt examples:

Prompt: "Based on my work experience and education, what skills do I excel in?"

ChatGPT can analyze your background and highlight your strongest skills, helping you understand where you shine. This could include technical skills, such as programming or data analysis, or soft skills, like communication or teamwork. You'll gain a clear picture of your existing abilities, allowing you to build upon them for career success.

Prompt: "What skills or areas should I focus on improving to advance in my career?"

ChatGPT can suggest specific areas for improvement based on your career goals and interests, ensuring targeted growth. For instance, if you aspire to a management role, ChatGPT might recommend improving your leadership, negotiation, or project management skills. Additionally, it can provide guidance on resources, such as online courses or workshops, to help you develop these skills effectively.

Prompt: "What are some relevant career opportunities or industries for my skillset?"

ChatGPT can recommend industries and job opportunities that align with your skills, making your job search more focused and efficient. This could involve suggesting positions in industries you may not have considered, opening up a world of new possibilities for your career. It can also help you tailor your resume and cover letter to highlight your most relevant skills for specific job applications.

In addition to the prompts above, consider engaging with ChatGPT to explore the following topics:

Skill gap analysis

ChatGPT can help you identify gaps in your skillset that may be holding you back from reaching your full potential in your chosen career. By understanding these gaps, you can create a targeted plan to develop those skills and become a more competitive candidate in the job market.

Prompt example: "What are the skill gaps I need to address to succeed in my desired career?"

Staying up-to-date with industry trends

ChatGPT can help you stay informed about emerging trends and skills in your chosen field. By staying current, you can ensure that your skillset remains relevant and valuable in the ever-evolving job market.

Prompt example: "What are the latest trends and skills in demand in the [industry]?"

Seeking mentorship and networking opportunities

ChatGPT can offer guidance on how to find mentors and network effectively within your industry. Building relationships with experienced professionals can provide invaluable insights, advice, and connections that can help you grow your skills and advance your career.

Prompt example: "How can I find a mentor and network effectively in my industry?"

By utilizing ChatGPT's capabilities, you can develop a deeper understanding of your current skills, identify areas for growth, and create a tailored plan for professional development. This will ultimately help you unlock your full potential and achieve success in your chosen career path.

Matching Your Personality and Preferences to Potential Career Paths

We'll wrap up by talking about how to use ChatGPT to match your interests and personality to potential job pathways. This technique can assist you in discovering a profession that not only fits your abilities and interests but also your distinct personality features, leading to a more rewarding and pleasurable working environment.

To match your personality to potential career paths, consider using a prompt like, *"Considering my personality traits and work preferences, what careers might be a good fit for me?"*

In order to provide a list of jobs that would be a good fit for you, ChatGPT analyzes your personality qualities, such as introversion or extroversion, and your work preferences, such as your need for structure or flexibility. For instance, ChatGPT may offer occupations in research, writing, or programming if you are an introverted person who prefers working alone. A prompt you can use for this would be *"What job roles align with my values, interests, and work style?"*

You can explore careers on ChatGPT that align with your beliefs, interests, and preferred working methods. You can pick a job that will be personally satisfying and fun by taking these aspects into account. For instance, ChatGPT might suggest jobs in non-profit organizations or social work if you prioritize social impact and have a collaborative work style. *"Which industries are best suited for my personality and preferences?"* is a good example of this.

ChatGPT can recommend industries that align with your personality and preferences, helping you find the right environment for your professional growth. For example, if you're a creative individual who thrives in fast-paced environments, ChatGPT might suggest industries such as advertising, media, or technology.

As you journey further into understanding your personality and preferences, it's essential to delve deeper into various aspects of your professional life. This introspection will help you make well-informed decisions about your career path. In this section, we'll explore three key areas: work environment preferences, work-life balance, and long-term career satisfaction.

ChatGPT can be a valuable resource, offering personalized insights and suggestions throughout this exploration.

Work Environment Preferences

Take a moment to reflect on your ideal work environment. Consider factors like company size, team dynamics, and office culture. Do you thrive in a large corporate setting or a small, close-knit team? Are you drawn to a traditional, structured environment or one that's more casual and laid-back?

ChatGPT can help you identify industries and companies that offer the type of environment you're most comfortable in and where you can excel. For example, you could ask ChatGPT *"Which industries or companies are known for having a collaborative, innovative, and flexible work environment?"*

Work-Life Balance

Another crucial aspect to consider is your desired work-life balance. Reflect on how important it is for you to maintain a balance between your professional and personal life, and how that aligns with your career choices.

ChatGPT can suggest careers or industries that offer the balance you're looking for, whether that's a traditional 9-to-5 schedule, remote work opportunities, or flexible hours. For example, you can ask ChatGPT, *"What careers or industries typically offer a healthy work-life balance with flexible scheduling options?"*

Long-term Career Satisfaction

Lastly, ponder your long-term career satisfaction. Think about factors like job stability, growth opportunities, and personal fulfillment. What kind of career will keep you engaged and satisfied over the years?

ChatGPT can help you evaluate potential career paths based on these criteria, ensuring you're on track to achieve lasting satisfaction in your professional life. To gather insights, you could use a prompt example: *"What are some stable careers with good growth opportunities that also provide a sense of personal fulfillment?"*

By examining these three areas with the help of ChatGPT, you'll gain a clearer understanding of your preferences and priorities. This self-knowledge will empower you to make informed decisions about your career, ultimately leading to a more fulfilling professional journey.

You will have a thorough understanding of how your personality and preferences might influence your employment choices by the end of this chapter. With ChatGPT's help, you'll be better equipped to discover the industries, employment responsibilities, and work environments that best suit your unique abilities, putting you on the path to a meaningful and successful professional career.

THREE

BUILDING YOUR PROFESSIONAL BRAND

~~~~~~~

We'll set off on a personal adventure to develop your professional identity in this chapter, with ChatGPT serving as your dependable travel partner. In today's competitive employment market, building a strong professional brand is critical. It is essential for demonstrating your distinct worth and leaving a lasting impression on potential employers.

We'll talk about how ChatGPT can help you write engaging resumes and cover letters that highlight your abilities and expertise. We'll also go over how to create a strong LinkedIn profile and online presence that will set you apart from your peers. We'll also learn how to use successful networking methods to broaden your network and open doors to new opportunities.

Remember that ChatGPT is here to help and guide you every step of the way as we traverse the realm of personal branding. With ChatGPT on your team, you will be well-equipped to create a professional brand that reflects your abilities, ambitions, and aspirations, paving the route to a rewarding and successful career.

Crafting an Effective Resume and Cover Letter

Your resume and cover letter are critical components of your job search strategy since they provide potential employers with an overview of your abilities, experience, and qualifications. In this section, we'll go through how ChatGPT may assist you in developing a resume and cover letter that effectively demonstrate your unique worth and leave a lasting impression on hiring managers.

ChatGPT can be your personal resume consultant, guiding you in structuring your resume to ensure it highlights your most relevant skills and accomplishments. You can ask ChatGPT for tips on resume formatting, content, and tailoring your resume to specific job postings. For instance, you can enter the prompt: *"What are some strategies for organizing my resume if I have extensive work experience in multiple fields?"* ChatGPT can then provide guidance on using a targeted resume format or grouping your experiences by skill set.

You could also request advice by asking: *"How can I effectively list my certifications and skills on my resume?"* ChatGPT will advise you on the best way to present your certifications and skills, ensuring they align with the job requirements and stand out to potential employers. Additionally, by asking, *"What are some tips for optimizing my resume for applicant tracking systems (ATS)?"*, ChatGPT can offer suggestions for making your resume ATS-friendly, such as using relevant keywords, simplifying your formatting, and avoiding images or graphics.

After you are done asking ways for ChatGPT to enhance your resume, you can then enter your entire resume and ask it to review it. ChatGPT will correct any grammatical or spelling errors and may also implement any additional information to help improve your overall resume. Don't be shy to ask for help, that's what this tool is here for!

When it comes to crafting a compelling cover letter, ChatGPT is ready to assist you in capturing your passion, enthusiasm, and suitability for a particular role. You can request advice on cover letter structure, content, and how to make a strong impression on potential employers. For example, you might ask ChatGPT: *"How can I effectively address the hiring manager in my cover letter if I don't know their name?"* ChatGPT can then provide recommendations for using a professional, gender-neutral salutation. You could also seek insights by asking *"What are some strategies for writing a cover letter when applying for a job in a different country?"* ChatGPT will offer advice on tailoring your cover letter for international job applications, including cultural considerations, language requirements, and relevant professional norms. Furthermore, by asking, *"How can I convey my enthusiasm for [Company name] mission and values in my cover letter?"*, ChatGPT can help you articulate your passion for a company's mission and values, ensuring your cover letter engages the reader and demonstrates your genuine interest in the organization.

By engaging with ChatGPT using these prompts and more, you'll be able to create a resume and cover letter that effectively showcase your unique strengths, experiences, and qualifications. With tailored guidance from ChatGPT, you can ensure that your application materials make a lasting impression on hiring managers, increasing your chances of landing the job you desire. This in-depth exploration of the resume and cover letter creation process will give you the tools and confidence to present yourself as the ideal candidate for any position.

Developing a Strong LinkedIn Profile and Online Presence

In today's digital world, your internet presence is crucial to your professional brand. In this section, we'll go through how to use ChatGPT to create a strong LinkedIn profile and maintain a consistent online presence across many platforms. We'll go over how to create an effective LinkedIn profile, manage your online reputation, and create content to support your professional identity.

A well-crafted LinkedIn profile serves as a cornerstone of your online presence, showcasing your skills, experience, and accomplishments to potential employers and industry connections. ChatGPT can offer suggestions on optimizing your LinkedIn profile to attract recruiters and make a lasting impression. For instance, you might ask ChatGPT: *"What are the key elements to include in my LinkedIn headline to effectively convey my unique value proposition?"* ChatGPT can then guide you in identifying the most important aspects of your professional identity to include in your headline, helping you stand out among your peers.

Additionally, you could inquire: *"How can I demonstrate my problem-solving abilities and leadership skills in my LinkedIn summary?"* ChatGPT can assist you in showcasing your unique strengths and achievements by providing examples and suggestions for incorporating these qualities into your summary. You might also seek guidance by asking: *"What are some tips for effectively listing my educational background and certifications on LinkedIn?"* In response, ChatGPT can provide advice on how to present your academic achievements and certifications, emphasizing their relevance to your career objectives and industry.

Furthermore, you can explore the potential of the 'Featured' section by asking *"How can I utilize the 'Featured' section of my LinkedIn profile to showcase my accomplishments and work samples?"* ChatGPT can recommend best practices for using the 'Featured' section to highlight your most impressive accomplishments, projects, or work samples, creating a visual representation of your professional capabilities.

By interacting with ChatGPT using these questions and others, you may build a LinkedIn profile that accurately reflects your qualifications, work history, and distinctive professional traits. Your web presence will become more substantial and reliable as a consequence, exposing your professional brand to potential employers and business contacts. You may take advantage of the power of online networking and position yourself as a highly sought-after candidate in your chosen industry by utilizing the strategies covered in this in-depth examination of LinkedIn profile optimization.

Consistent Online Presence

Maintaining a cohesive and professional online presence across various platforms is essential for reinforcing your personal brand. ChatGPT can help you ensure that your personal brand is consistent and aligned with your career goals. For example, you might ask ChatGPT, *"How can I create a content strategy for my professional blog that aligns with my personal brand and industry expertise?"* In response, ChatGPT can help you develop a content plan that showcases your knowledge and insights, positioning you as a thought leader and attracting potential employers or clients.

Another way to enhance your online presence is by utilizing social media platforms such as Twitter. You could inquire, *"How can I effectively use Twitter for professional networking and personal branding in my industry?"* ChatGPT can offer advice on leveraging Twitter for networking, engaging with industry influencers, and sharing valuable content that reflects your expertise and personal brand.

To further showcase your professional achievements, you might ask, *"What are some ways to showcase my professional achievements and expertise on platforms like GitHub or Behance?"* ChatGPT can provide guidance on using portfolio-based platforms to highlight your skills and accomplishments, demonstrating your professional abilities to potential employers or clients.

Moreover, you can explore opportunities to participate in podcasts or webinars to expand your professional network and enhance your personal brand. You might ask, *"How can I use podcasts or webinars to expand my professional network and enhance my personal brand?"* ChatGPT can recommend strategies for participating in podcasts or webinars as a speaker or guest, leveraging these platforms to share your expertise and connect with industry professionals.

By thoroughly exploring these topics, you'll gain a more comprehensive understanding of how to use ChatGPT to optimize your online presence and maintain a consistent personal brand. These insights will help you develop a strong professional brand that will resonate with potential employers and industry contacts, positioning you for greater career success.

FOUR

MASTERING THE JOB SEARCH

~~~~~~~

The job search process can be difficult to navigate, but with the right strategies and tools, you can make it more manageable and successful. We will look at how ChatGPT can help you find job openings, identify the best platforms and resources for your industry, and stay organized and motivated throughout the job search process in this chapter. You'll be better prepared to land your dream job if you use ChatGPT as your job search companion.

Utilizing ChatGPT to Find Job Openings and Opportunities

The first step in a successful job search is to find the right job openings. ChatGPT can help you identify relevant job opportunities by providing you with up-to-date information and insights on the job market. For instance, you could ask ChatGPT: *"What are some popular job boards or websites for finding job openings in [your industry]?"* ChatGPT can provide you with a list of job boards or websites specific to your industry, streamlining your job search and ensuring you have access to the most relevant opportunities.

Another question you might pose is, *"How can I stay updated on new job opportunities in my field?"* ChatGPT can suggest strategies for staying informed about the latest job openings, such as signing up for job alerts, following industry news, or joining professional online forums.

In addition to helping you find job openings, ChatGPT can tailor your job search to your specific skills, preferences, and goals. This will ensure that you apply to positions that align with your unique qualifications. For example, you could ask, *"What are some job titles or roles that would be a good fit for my skills and experience?"* Based on your background, ChatGPT can recommend job titles or roles that suit your skillset and experience, helping you focus your job search on the most relevant opportunities.

You might also ask, *"Based on my career goals and values, what kinds of businesses or organizations should I think about applying to?"* The possibility of long-term employment happiness rises when ChatGPT analyzes your professional goals and values and suggests businesses or organizations that support your aspirations.

Identifying the Best Platforms and Resources for Your Industry

Different industries have unique job search platforms and resources. ChatGPT can help you identify the best platforms and resources for your industry, making your job search more efficient and effective. To uncover these resources, ask questions like, *"What are some industry-specific job search websites for [your industry]?"* ChatGPT can provide a list of job search websites tailored to your industry, ensuring that you have access to the most relevant job listings.

Another question to consider is: *"Are there any professional organizations or networking groups in my field that I should join to find job opportunities?"* ChatGPT can recommend professional organizations and networking groups related to your field. Joining these groups can not only help you find job opportunities but also expand your professional network and learn from industry experts.

Additionally, you might ask ChatGPT, *"What are some reputable industry publications or websites that I should follow to stay informed about trends and developments in my field?"* By staying informed about your industry, you'll be better prepared for job interviews and be able to identify emerging job opportunities.

You can also inquire about industry-specific job fairs and events by asking, *"What are some upcoming job fairs or networking events in my industry that I should attend?"* ChatGPT can help you find relevant events in your area or online, allowing you to connect with potential employers and gain valuable insights into your industry.

Another resource to explore is online courses and certifications related to your field. Try asking, *"What are some popular online courses or certifications that can help boost my career in [your industry]?"* ChatGPT can recommend courses or certifications that could enhance your skillset, making you a more attractive candidate to potential employers.

Lastly, consider asking ChatGPT about social media strategies for your industry: *"How can I effectively use social media platforms like LinkedIn, Twitter, or Instagram to connect with professionals and find job opportunities in [your industry]?"* ChatGPT can offer tips on using social media to network, engage with industry influencers, and share valuable content that reflects your expertise and personal brand.

You'll have a more thorough and tailored approach to your job hunt in your particular industry by utilizing ChatGPT's support while you explore these many platforms and resources. By doing this, you'll increase your chances of landing the perfect employment opportunity, grow your professional network, and keep current with market trends.

Organizing Your Job Search and Staying Motivated Throughout the Process

Staying organized and motivated during your job search is crucial for success. ChatGPT can offer guidance on organizing your job search as well as strategies for staying motivated. For example, you could ask, *"What are some strategies for organizing and prioritizing job applications?"* ChatGPT can suggest practical ways to keep track of your job applications, such as using spreadsheets or project management tools, making it easier to monitor your progress and follow up on applications.

You might also input the prompt, *"How can I set up a daily or weekly job search routine?"* ChatGPT can help you establish a job search routine that fits your schedule and ensures consistent effort. This could include setting aside specific times each day or week for job searching, networking, and updating your application materials.

Maintaining motivation throughout the job search process is equally important. ChatGPT can provide encouragement, advice, and strategies to help you stay motivated and focused on your goals. For instance, you could ask, *"What are some ways to stay motivated during a lengthy job search?"* ChatGPT can offer suggestions for maintaining motivation, such as setting short-term goals, celebrating small successes, and connecting with supportive individuals who can provide encouragement and guidance.

Another prompt to consider is, *"How can I keep a positive mindset and avoid burnout while looking for a job?"* ChatGPT can provide tips on maintaining a positive mindset, like practicing gratitude, focusing on your strengths, and taking breaks when needed to recharge and refocus.

You might also explore ways to develop new skills and enhance your employability during your job search. Asking ChatGPT, *"What are some valuable skills I can learn or improve on to increase my chances of finding a job in [your industry]?"* can result in suggestions for relevant skills or courses that can enhance your career prospects.

By the end of this chapter, you'll have a thorough understanding of how to use ChatGPT to effectively master the job search process. With its guidance and support, you'll be well-equipped to navigate the job market and locate your dream career in your chosen industry. Remember to use ChatGPT as a helpful resource and companion as you move through your job search journey, giving insights, encouragement, and motivation to help you reach your professional goals.

FIVE

ACING THE INTERVIEW PROCESS

~~~~~~

The many ways ChatGPT can help you master the interview process, from the early stages of preparation all the way through to post-interview follow-up, are covered in this chapter. The advice from ChatGPT will give you the skills you need to approach interviews with confidence, whether they're in-person, over the phone, or even on a panel, and will ultimately help you get the job you've been aiming for.

We'll go through topics including comprehending different types of interview questions, making a strong impression in every interview environment, and effectively expressing your unique qualifications. ChatGPT will provide vital insights and resources throughout this trip to boost your confidence and ensure you're well-prepared for any obstacles that may emerge during the interview.

We'll also go through ways of dealing with interview-related tension and anxiety, as well as techniques for maintaining a cheerful and professional demeanor throughout the process. ChatGPT will be your trusted ally as you navigate the complicated and often nerve-racking world of interviews, providing help and direction at every level.

You'll have a vast toolkit of useful advice, tactics, and insights from ChatGPT by the end of this chapter, giving you everything you need to ace the interview. You'll be equipped to handle any interview setting with conviction and poise while showcasing your qualifications for the position you want.

Preparing for Interviews

To kick things off, let's talk about how ChatGPT can be your personal guide in preparing for interviews by offering insights and advice on a wide range of interview questions. When you practice with ChatGPT, you'll not only gain confidence but also become more at ease in answering various questions that may come your way.

ChatGPT is here to help you with general questions like "How do I craft the perfect response to *'Tell me about yourself?'"*, *"What's a positive way to discuss my weaknesses during an interview?"*, or *"What's the best approach to explaining gaps in my employment history?"* But that's not all! ChatGPT can also support you with more specific queries tailored to your industry or the position you're applying for. For example, if you're applying for a marketing role, you might ask, *"How can I showcase my creativity and marketing expertise during the interview?"*

Regardless of the interview format or the company you're aiming for, this individualized advice will make sure you're ready to discuss your special strengths and experiences. You can be sure that you're presenting yourself in the best possible light in every interview situation when using AI.

Tips for Remote and In-Person Interviews

Next, let's get into some tips and strategies for excelling in both remote and in-person interviews. ChatGPT is here to offer you personalized advice on how to present yourself professionally and confidently in any situation.

For remote video interviews, ask ChatGPT, *"How can I ensure my remote interview setup is professional and distraction-free?"* It will provide you with valuable advice on the ideal camera angle, appropriate lighting, and ways to minimize any distractions during your interview. You could also ask, *"What's the best way to convey enthusiasm and energy during a remote interview?"* In response, ChatGPT will guide you on maintaining eye contact, using expressive body language, and modulating your voice to keep the conversation engaging.

When it comes to in-person interviews, enter the prompt, *"How should I dress for an interview in a creative industry?"* ChatGPT will offer you specific suggestions on how to dress professionally while still showcasing your personal style, taking into account the culture and norms of the industry you're targeting. You might also ask, *"How can I build a connection with my interviewer?"* ChatGPT will help you understand the importance of positive non-verbal cues, such as a confident handshake, a genuine smile, and maintaining eye contact, as well as providing advice on small talk and active listening techniques to build rapport with your interviewer.

Remember, you can personalize your prompts even more by entering the name of the company or industry you are targeting. By using AI, you'll be well-equipped to make a strong first impression on your interviewer whether you're speaking in-person or over the phone by adopting these strategies. Never forget that ChatGPT is here to support you through the entire interviewing process, offering individualized counsel and direction based on your particular requirements and goals.

Handling Behavioral, Situational, and Technical Interview Questions

In this section, we'll delve deeper into how ChatGPT can help you tackle various types of interview questions, including behavioral, situational, and technical, all while using a more personal tone to connect with your unique experiences and aspirations.

When it comes to behavioral questions, ChatGPT is here to guide you through the STAR method and also help you uncover a variety of experiences from your past that highlight your abilities in different scenarios. For example, you can ask ChatGPT, *"Can you help me think of a time when I demonstrated strong teamwork skills in a challenging situation?"* By engaging with ChatGPT in this manner, you'll receive personalized guidance that enables you to showcase your strengths more effectively during the interview.

For situational questions, ChatGPT aims to offer insights into the interviewer's objectives, helping you understand and address the underlying concerns behind the questions. You can approach ChatGPT with prompts like, *"How can I show my adaptability and problem-solving skills when faced with a tight deadline and limited resources?"* ChatGPT will help you brainstorm ideas, consider various perspectives, and ultimately demonstrate your ability to think on your feet and adapt to new challenges.

When it comes to technical questions, ChatGPT is your go-to resource for identifying learning materials, suggesting practice exercises, and even providing guidance on tackling questions outside your area of expertise, all while maintaining confidence and composure. Feel free to ask ChatGPT questions like, *"What are some strategies for staying calm and focused when faced with a complex technical problem during an interview?"* or *"How can I convey my willingness to learn and grow when I encounter a technical question that I'm not familiar with?"* With using this tool, you'll stand out from the rest and be better prepared to handle technical questions with grace and poise, even when they're outside your comfort zone.

By interacting with ChatGPT on a more personal level, you will be able to obtain personalized advice and assistance that resonates with your particular experiences, making your interview preparation more effective and helping you shine throughout the process.

Post-Interview Follow-up and Thank-You Notes

As we wrap up this chapter, let's talk about the significance of post-interview follow-up and the art of crafting heartfelt thank-you notes. ChatGPT is here to help you compose genuine, personalized messages that will leave a memorable, positive impression on your interviewer. For instance, you can input the prompt, *"Help me express my gratitude and enthusiasm in a thank-you note from my recent interview for XXXX position."* ChatGPT can guide you through the process, emphasizing the importance of timeliness, personalization, and genuine enthusiasm.

You could also inquire, *"What are some creative ways to follow up after an interview if I haven't heard back within the expected timeframe?"* ChatGPT will offer thoughtful advice on striking the perfect balance between showing your continued interest in the position and respecting the interviewer's time. It might suggest sending a relevant article, asking a thoughtful question about the company, or even providing an update on a recent accomplishment or experience that further highlights your suitability for the role.

Another important aspect of post-interview follow-up is maintaining professional relationships with interviewers, even if you're not offered the job. You can ask ChatGPT, *"How can I continue to engage with an interviewer in a meaningful way, despite not being selected for the position?"* ChatGPT will provide helpful suggestions, such as connecting on LinkedIn, periodically sharing updates on your career progress, or even asking for feedback on your interview performance. Remember, these connections can be invaluable for future opportunities, and nurturing them can pave the way for exciting new prospects down the line.

By focusing on these post-interview follow-up strategies, you will not only leave a positive impression on your interviewers, but you will also demonstrate your commitment to building professional relationships. You may create a powerful and personal follow-up strategy with ChatGPT's assistance that keeps you in the minds of potential employers and industry contacts, building the framework for future success.

SIX

PROFESSIONAL DEVELOPMENT & SKILL-BUILDING

~~~~~~

In the dynamic landscape of today's job market, the key to success lies not just in adapting, but also in anticipating change and evolving proactively. Now, more than ever, it's crucial to commit to lifelong learning and continuous professional development. As we journey together through this chapter, we'll see just how your AI companion can be a vital ally in this endeavor.

We'll uncover chances for growth that correspond with your career goals, identify skills you can improve or learn new ones, and keep on top of developing trends in your area. ChatGPT is more than a tool; it is a consultant who gives personalized insights to help you stay competitive and relevant.

Furthermore, we will navigate the huge universe of professional development materials. From online courses and certificates to hands-on workshops, ChatGPT will direct you to the ones that are most relevant to your learning style and professional objectives.

But the journey doesn't stop there. ChatGPT will also be by your side as you incorporate these new skills into your professional narrative, whether that's enhancing your resume, updating your LinkedIn profile, or applying your newfound knowledge to real-world situations.

By the end of this chapter, you'll see how ChatGPT empowers you to take control of your professional development, helping you not just keep pace with the current job market, but stay a step ahead of its ever-evolving demands. Together, we'll not just meet the challenges of today, but prepare to seize the opportunities of tomorrow.

Using ChatGPT to Find Online Courses, Workshops, and Certifications

Online learning provides limitless options for professional development in our ever-changing digital world. However, with so many courses, workshops, and certifications available, selecting the perfect one can be difficult. Let's look at how ChatGPT may be your personal guide on this journey, assisting you in locating the best resources to advance your profession.

Finding the perfect online course can be tricky with all the options available. But don't worry; ChatGPT is here to help. Ask it something like, *"Can you recommend top-rated online courses for data science?"* or *"Which platforms offer the best project management courses?"* With ChatGPT's guidance, the right course is just a prompt away.

Workshops offer hands-on, interactive experiences that can enrich your skills. And yes, ChatGPT can assist you in finding the right ones. Try asking, *"Are there any engaging workshops for improving public speaking?"* or *"Can you suggest beginner-friendly coding workshops?"* ChatGPT can point you towards workshops that not only enhance your skills but also provide networking opportunities.

Certifications can give your career a significant boost, showcasing your expertise and commitment to learning. Ask ChatGPT, *"What are the key certifications for a cybersecurity career?"* or *"How can I prepare for the PMP certification?"* With its guidance, you'll discover recognized certifications in your field and the resources to ace the exams.

Remember, online learning isn't just about finding resources; it's about effectively utilizing them. Ask ChatGPT for tips like, *"How can I stay motivated while learning online?"*

Remember, online learning isn't just about finding resources; it's about effectively utilizing them. Ask ChatGPT for tips like, *"How can I stay motivated while learning online?"* or *"What strategies work best for online learning?"*

Make the most of these prospects for job improvement by embracing this section and utilizing ChatGPT as your own navigator through the enormous ocean of online learning.

Identifying Relevant Learning Platforms

Navigating the abundance of online learning platforms can seem overwhelming, but fret not, ChatGPT is here to simplify this for you. It's adept at helping you unearth platforms that dovetail perfectly with your industry, your present skill set, and even your individual learning style.

Suppose you're a budding software developer eager to refine your skillset. With the multitude of platforms out there, knowing where to begin can be a challenge. You could consult ChatGPT, asking, *"Which online learning platforms are ideal for boosting my skills in full-stack development?"* Drawing from its extensive knowledge, ChatGPT can curate a list of platforms tailored to your needs, such as freeCodeCamp for hands-on practice, Coursera for structured courses by top universities, or Udacity for more in-depth, project-based learning.

Let's take another scenario. Perhaps your interests lie in a niche discipline like Quantum Computing. You could ask, *"What are the best resources for learning Quantum Computing online?"* ChatGPT can guide you towards platforms or courses that offer high-quality content in this specialized field, ensuring your learning aligns with your specific aspirations.

Or consider a situation where you're a newcomer to the realm of machine learning. You might query, *"What online platforms offer the best introductory courses in machine learning?"* ChatGPT can suggest platforms known for their user-friendly approach to complex concepts, like Kaggle for hands-on practice with datasets, or edX for courses by top institutions like MIT or Harvard.

ChatGPT's personalized guidance extends beyond mere platform recommendations. It can also provide advice on how to maximize your learning experience, manage your study schedule, and track your progress. For example, you can ask, *"What strategies can help me stay motivated during a self-paced online course?"* or *"What's the best way to apply what I've learned from an online course to real-world projects?"*

This expanded part will show you how ChatGPT, with its contextual, individualized responses, may act as an excellent mentor, guiding you through the vast world of online learning. ChatGPT is ready to help you on your path to professional progress, whether you're a beginner, intermediate learner, or advanced professional.

Finding Courses Tailored to Your Experience Level

Navigating the online learning world can be difficult, especially when trying to match your ability level with an appropriate course. It is critical to choose a course that neither undershoots nor overshoots your talents, but instead gives exactly the appropriate degree of challenge to maximize your learning potential. ChatGPT may be a helpful guide in this process, directing you to courses that complement your present expertise and talents.

Let's say you're keen on exploring the fascinating world of data analysis, but you're unsure where to begin. You could lean on ChatGPT for guidance and ask, *"ChatGPT, could you suggest some introductory courses on data analysis suitable for beginners?"* Responding to your query, ChatGPT can present you with a meticulously curated list of foundational data analysis courses perfect for beginners. These selections ensure you establish a strong base before you delve into more intricate subjects.

But the assistance from ChatGPT extends beyond just course recommendations. It can help demystify the course structure and prerequisites, preparing you well in advance. For instance, you might inquire: *"ChatGPT, what kind of prerequisites should I know before embarking on this data analysis course?"* or *"What sort of projects or assignments might this data analysis course involve?"*

As you advance in your data analysis journey, ChatGPT can continue to provide valuable guidance. For instance, after completing a beginner's course, you might ask, *"ChatGPT, what are some intermediate-level data analysis courses I should consider next?"* This way, ChatGPT assists in sculpting a clear learning path, ensuring a seamless transition between different skill levels, and facilitating continuous learning.

Once you've acquired new skills and completed courses, ChatGPT can guide you on how to effectively highlight these accomplishments on your professional platforms. You could ask, *"ChatGPT, help me articulate my newly acquired data analysis skills on my LinkedIn profile or resume."* With such holistic guidance, ChatGPT doesn't just facilitate your learning—it propels your professional growth.

Evaluating Course Quality and Instructor Expertise

Given the large range of courses offered, quality assurance is critical when stepping into the world of online learning. Making an educated selection might be difficult due to disparities in instructional quality, course content, and teacher skill. ChatGPT may be a valuable ally in this process, assisting you in dissecting and evaluating the different factors that influence course quality and teacher ability.

Suppose you're interested in the rapidly evolving field of machine learning and are looking for a course to enroll in. You can use the prompt, *"What steps should I take to assess the quality of a potential machine learning course before signing up?"* In response, ChatGPT can guide you through a systematic approach to course evaluation.

This might include checking student reviews and ratings, a valuable source of insights into the course's effectiveness and practicality. ChatGPT can guide you on how to interpret these reviews, spotting patterns of praise or criticism that might inform your decision.

Furthermore, ChatGPT can advise you on how to scrutinize the course syllabus or curriculum. You might pose the question: *"What should I look for in a machine learning course syllabus to ensure it covers relevant topics and has comprehensive content?"* The AI can then provide a rundown of key topics a high-quality machine learning course should cover, helping you assess the course's thoroughness and relevance to your learning objectives.

The instructor's background and expertise significantly influence the course's quality. Here, ChatGPT can help you evaluate the instructor's credentials and teaching style. For example, you could ask, *"What qualifications and experience should an instructor of a machine learning course possess?"* or *"How can I understand the teaching style of an instructor before enrolling in the course?"*

Finally, as you advance in your learning journey, you might need guidance on advanced courses or specialized tracks in machine learning. For such queries, you could say, *"What are some high-quality advanced courses in machine learning, and what factors should I consider before enrolling?"* By implementing ChatGPT into your course selection process, you can guarantee that your time, effort, and resources are invested in high-quality courses with strong learning results.

Maximizing the Value of Your Learning Experience

Making the most of your online learning experience takes more than just viewing lecture videos and reading course materials. Active engagement, frequent practice, and a well-structured learning plan can all help you learn more effectively. In this section, we'll look at how ChatGPT can help you use these tactics to get the most out of your online education, especially if you're taking a course like marketing.

You might start with a question like, *"How can I set clear, achievable goals for my marketing course?"* ChatGPT can then help you outline SMART (Specific, Measurable, Achievable, Relevant, Time-bound) goals that align with your learning objectives and career aspirations. These could include understanding key marketing concepts, mastering specific digital marketing tools, or even applying the course knowledge to improve the marketing strategy of your own business.

As you progress through the course, staying organized and managing your time effectively can be challenging. To overcome this, you might ask, *"Can you give me tips on organizing my study schedule for the online marketing course?"* In response, ChatGPT can provide you with strategies for breaking down the course content into manageable chunks, scheduling regular study sessions, and maintaining a balance between learning and practice.

Active engagement is a vital aspect of online learning. You might inquire, *"How can I actively participate and engage in my marketing course to enhance my understanding?"* ChatGPT can then offer suggestions such as participating in forum discussions, connecting with peers for group study sessions, or reaching out to the instructor with specific questions or for further clarification on complex topics.

Applying what you learn to real-world scenarios can immensely boost your understanding and retention. Try asking, *"What are some practical projects or scenarios where I can apply my knowledge from the marketing course?"* ChatGPT can then propose various hands-on projects, like creating a marketing campaign for a hypothetical product or analyzing the marketing strategy of a successful company.

Lastly, upon course completion, you might want to showcase your newly acquired skills.

You could ask, *"How can I showcase the skills I gained from the marketing course on my LinkedIn profile or resume?"* ChatGPT can provide advice on how to highlight your new skills, completed projects, and the impact of your learning on your professional capabilities.

You'll have a thorough grasp of how ChatGPT can enhance your online learning experience, making it more immersive, engaging, and ultimately more advantageous for your career advancement, by the time this investigation is complete. You'll be able to choose the most pertinent courses and get the most out of them with ChatGPT as your learning partner, putting you on the road to ongoing professional development.

Developing New Skills to Stay Competitive in Your Industry

Maintaining competitiveness in a job market that is constantly changing calls for a proactive approach to skill development. Your professional value will increase and your industry relevance will be maintained if you keep learning new skills and developing your expertise. The most important skills to learn can be identified and prioritized with ChatGPT, according to your unique professional path.

One way to begin is by asking ChatGPT about the latest trends and advancements in your industry. This knowledge will provide you with the necessary context to understand which skills are currently in demand and which ones might be emerging as essential in the near future. For example, you might ask, *"What are the current trends in cybersecurity, and what skills should I develop to stay competitive?"*

Another crucial aspect of staying competitive is understanding how technology impacts your field. ChatGPT can offer insights into the latest tools, software, and platforms relevant to your industry. By keeping up with technological advancements, you'll be better equipped to adapt to new ways of working and leverage these tools to improve your performance. You could ask ChatGPT, *"What new tools or technologies are shaping the future of finance, and how can I learn to use them effectively?"*

Additionally, consider using ChatGPT to explore complementary skills that could broaden your capabilities and make you a more versatile professional. For instance, if you're a software developer, learning about user experience (UX) design can help you create more user-friendly applications. To discover such complementary skills, try asking ChatGPT, *"What skills can I learn to complement my existing expertise as a software developer?"*

Lastly, don't overlook the importance of honing your soft skills, such as communication, leadership, and emotional intelligence. These skills are highly valued across various industries and can significantly contribute to your career success. ChatGPT can provide you with resources, tips, and techniques to improve your soft skills, making you a more well-rounded professional. To explore this further, ask ChatGPT, *"What are some effective strategies to improve my leadership skills?"*

You'll be better equipped to handle new problems, adjust to changes, and ultimately stay competitive in your sector by developing the skills that are most pertinent to your industry and work role. You'll be able to choose the most crucial skills to improve and locate the resources to study them with ChatGPT as your career coach, assuring your professional growth and success.

Strategies for Continuous Learning and Growth

A commitment to ongoing learning and continuous improvement is necessary to successfully navigate the rapidly evolving professional landscape of today. We'll go together through a variety of tactics in this comprehensive exploration to keep you motivated, fortify your commitment, and keep you moving forward in your learning. We will make sure that you continue to be a dynamic actor in determining your own professional path, rather than merely a participant.

Building a Personal Learning Network

Building a personal learning network (PLN) is like planting your own career garden. Each connection represents a seed that, with time and nurturing, can grow into a flourishing relationship, offering inspiration, advice, and potential collaboration opportunities. Your PLN becomes your community, your sounding board, and your cheerleading squad, all supporting your growth in your chosen field.

As your assistant, ChatGPT is here to lend a helping hand in creating this network. Just imagine walking into a bustling virtual room filled with experts and enthusiasts in your field, say, data science. Where do you start? What do you say? You can start with the prompt, *"Where can I find online communities to connect with data science professionals?"* This can introduce you to the popular forums, LinkedIn groups, or Twitter spaces where data science conversations are happening. It can even point out influential data scientists you might want to follow for their thought-provoking posts.

But it's not just about making connections; it's also about cultivating these relationships. You could ask: *"What are some effective ways to engage with professionals and thought leaders in the data science community on LinkedIn?"* ChatGPT can guide you through the etiquette of online engagement, from commenting meaningfully on posts to sharing relevant content and even reaching out for informational interviews.

Perhaps you've found a potential mentor or industry expert you'd like to approach. You might ask ChatGPT: *"How should I approach a potential mentor within my field?"* This prompt can provide advice on crafting a respectful, compelling message that shows your genuine interest and eagerness to learn.

By the end of this journey, with ChatGPT's help, you'll not only have a strong PLN, but you'll also know how to nurture it, making it an invaluable asset in your career. This network will keep you in touch with industry trends, offer diverse perspectives, and provide opportunities for lifelong learning, helping you thrive in your career and stay ahead of the game.

Time Management and Goal Setting

On the journey of continuous learning, you're the captain of your ship, and effective time management and goal setting are your compass and map, directing you toward success. In the midst of a vast sea of knowledge, it's easy to become overwhelmed or lose sight of your ultimate goal. That's where you can use your AI assistant which is ready to assist you in effectively charting your course.

ChatGPT can assist you in setting SMART goals - those that are Specific, Measurable, Achievable, Relevant, and Time-bound. These goals give clarity to your learning journey, transforming a vague notion of 'I want to learn more' into a clear, actionable plan like 'I want to complete an online course in data analytics within three months to enhance my job performance.'

You might ask ChatGPT, *"How do I set SMART goals for my professional development?"* In response, ChatGPT could guide you through each aspect of a SMART goal, helping you create a personalized, achievable learning plan tailored to your aspirations and circumstances.

But even the best-laid plans can go awry without effective time management. Whether you're balancing professional development with a full-time job or navigating a career transition, managing your time well is crucial. ChatGPT can introduce you to a variety of time management strategies and techniques, helping you find what works best for you.

For instance, you might prompt ChatGPT with, *"What are some time management strategies that can help me stay on track with my professional development goals?"* ChatGPT could suggest tried-and-true techniques like the Pomodoro Technique, where you work in focused bursts with regular breaks to enhance productivity. It might recommend time-blocking, a method where you dedicate specific blocks of time to different tasks throughout your day. Or, it could introduce you to prioritization methods, helping you distinguish between urgent and important tasks to prevent burnout and maintain progress.

By adopting these strategies with the assistance of ChatGPT, you will not only sail smoothly on your journey of continuous learning, but you will also enjoy the journey, confident in your ability to navigate the waves of professional development.

Embracing a Growth Mindset

A positive perspective serves as a guide as you navigate the complicated terrain of professional development. Adopting a growth mindset, or the empowering conviction that abilities and intelligence can be developed through commitment and effort, is the key. This way of thinking encourages resilience, adaptability, and lifelong learning, all of which are necessary for success in our constantly changing environment.

A positive perspective serves as a guide as you navigate the complicated terrain of professional development. Adopting a growth mindset, or the empowering conviction that abilities and intelligence can be developed through commitment and effort, is the key. This way of thinking encourages resilience, adaptability, and lifelong learning, all of which are necessary for success in our constantly changing environment.

Suppose you find yourself grappling with a challenging task at work, feeling like you're hitting a wall. Here's where you can lean on ChatGPT. By asking, *"I'm stuck with a tough challenge at work. How can I use a growth mindset to navigate this?"* ChatGPT can guide you to reframe the challenge as an opportunity and provide strategies to break down the task, learn from setbacks, and persistently push forward.

If you're eager to foster a growth mindset but unsure of where to start, ChatGPT is there to help. When you ask, *"What are some practical strategies for cultivating a growth mindset?"* it can offer actionable tips. These might include setting learning goals, seeking constructive feedback, embracing failures as learning opportunities, and celebrating incremental progress. ChatGPT can also suggest mindfulness techniques to bolster self-awareness and resilience.

In case you're wondering how to stay motivated and committed to continuous learning, you can turn to ChatGPT. By asking, *"How can I stay motivated and committed to continuous learning?"* It can suggest tactics like finding your learning 'why', tracking your progress, leveraging varied learning resources, and finding a balance between the pursuit of mastery and the joy of exploration.

By the end of this journey, you'll have a solid grasp of the power of a growth mindset and its role in lifelong learning. You'll also appreciate how ChatGPT can be a helpful companion, assisting you in confronting problems, seizing opportunities, and constantly striving for growth and learning. With a growth mindset and the help of ChatGPT, you'll be able to uncover new potentials, adapt to an ever-changing professional scene, and fuel your journey toward your career goals.

Learning from Failure

The path to professional development is rarely a straight one; it is frequently defined by setbacks, detours, and, yes, even failures. On the other hand, recognizing that these failures are not fatal but rather a normal and necessary part of the learning process can inspire in you the bravery to take risks and the resilience to learn from your mistakes.

ChatGPT is here to help you perceive these instances as stepping stones toward your ultimate success, not as hurdles. It might help you view failure as a springboard for development and learning, rather than a final condition. It helps you reflect on your experiences, identify areas for growth, and chart a course of action for the future.

For instance, if you've recently experienced a project setback and are unsure how to proceed, ChatGPT can be a valuable resource. You might ask, *"I've recently had a project that didn't go as planned. How can I use this experience as a tool for learning and growth?"* In response, ChatGPT will guide you through a reflective process, helping you dissect the experience, identify key lessons, and develop an actionable plan for future projects.

Moreover, it's crucial to remember that failure often brings with it a heavy emotional toll. ChatGPT is also here to assist you with managing this emotional aspect. By asking, *"I'm feeling demotivated after a recent failure. How can I regain my confidence and move forward?"* ChatGPT will offer empathetic advice to help you process your feelings, regain your confidence, and reignite your motivation.

Such discussions will educate you to accept failure as a useful teacher, building resilience and adaptation. Failure will not be a debilitating force, but rather a transforming one, driving you to better methods and greater progress. By the conclusion of this trip, you'll be well-equipped to deal with setbacks and disappointments in your professional life, transforming them into significant learning opportunities while constantly moving forward toward your goals.

Staying Curious and Open-Minded

Cultivating and sustaining a feeling of curiosity, as well as an open mind, are essential for lifelong learning and professional development. In an ever-changing world, your capacity to actively seek out and welcome new experiences, ideas, and views is a game changer. With this expanded perspective, you can adjust to the ever-changing dynamics of your business and profession with agility and foresight.

ChatGPT is eager to serve as your personal coach in cultivating curiosity and an open mind throughout your professional path. It can recommend a variety of strategies to excite your curiosity and broaden your horizons, such as visiting industry events and participating in webinars, as well as digging into a wide range of books and articles that go outside the bounds of your sector.

For example, suppose you're eager to fuel your intellectual curiosity but unsure where to start. By asking ChatGPT, *"What are some activities or resources that can help me stay curious and open-minded in my career?"* It can provide a curated list of diverse options tailored to your interests and schedule. These may include recommendations for top-rated industry webinars, thought-provoking books, stimulating podcasts, or influential thought leaders to follow on social media.

Moreover, engaging with a variety of professionals and thinkers is a great way to expose yourself to diverse perspectives and fresh ideas. If you're looking for ways to connect with professionals outside your immediate network, ChatGPT can help. When you ask, *"How can I engage with diverse professionals in my field?"*, this prompt can offer suggestions like participating in LinkedIn group discussions, attending networking events, or even joining online forums specific to your industry.

You'll see firsthand how curiosity and an open mind can spark lifelong learning and support your professional development during this exploration. ChatGPT will be your dependable travel buddy, providing insightful advice and useful materials to stoke your interest and broaden your horizons. You'll find yourself ready and eager to handle the ever-changing work world as you grow these skills with ChatGPT by your side. It's a thrilling path filled with ongoing learning, personal development, and pushing the limits of what you once believed was achievable in your profession.

Accountability and Support Systems

A strong combination of motivation, dedication, and a supportive environment is at the heart of continual learning. Setting lofty professional development objectives is one thing, but without a solid accountability mechanism, it's all too easy for these goals to fall between the cracks. This is where ChatGPT comes in, providing advice and techniques for establishing an effective accountability and support structure.

Imagine you've set a goal to upskill in a new area. You're excited, yet a bit daunted by the road ahead. With ChatGPT, you can ask, *"How can I set up an accountability system to keep me on track with my professional development goals?"* In response, ChatGPT can provide strategies tailored to your unique needs. These might include finding an accountability partner who shares similar goals, joining or forming a mastermind group for collective growth and learning, or using goal-setting and tracking apps to monitor your progress.

Similarly, if you're feeling isolated in your learning journey, ChatGPT can help. When you ask, *"How can I build a supportive learning environment to help me grow professionally?"* it can suggest ways to leverage your personal learning network. You could engage in online learning communities, seek mentorship, or regularly share your learning updates with colleagues or peers for encouragement and constructive feedback.

But it's not just about setting up systems. ChatGPT can also help you maintain these systems effectively. By entering, *"How can I maintain my accountability and support system effectively?"* it can offer tips like setting regular check-ins with your accountability partner, actively participating in your mastermind groups, and giving back to your learning community through knowledge sharing and peer support.

In the end, it comes down to incorporating these tactics into your daily routine and developing an attitude of constant learning and progress. With this dedication and ChatGPT as your guide, you will be able to negotiate the volatile landscape of your industry with resilience and agility. You're not just preparing for your current employment, but also for future prospects. It's about committing to a lifelong path of learning, curiosity, and growth—essential factors for long-term success in your professional aspirations.

SEVEN

NAVIGATING CAREER TRANSITIONS

~~~~~~~

In the kaleidoscope of life, changing careers stands out as one of the most exciting yet intimidating crossroads. It's a thrilling journey, colored by self-discovery, personal growth, and ripe with opportunities. However, this journey, as enticing as it is, isn't devoid of its share of challenges. There's the specter of uncertainty that looms large, coupled with a sense of anxiety that's hard to shake off. But, like every great adventure, having a reliable ally by your side can make all the difference.

We're here to walk you through the maze of career change in this chapter, step by step. ChatGPT is prepared to give insights, guidance, and resources catered to your particular requirements, from evaluating your transferable abilities and viable career routes to preparing for interviews in a new sector and negotiating employment offers.

We'll also look at how ChatGPT may help you cope with the emotional ups and downs that come with changing careers. It can offer advice on how to overcome anxiety about the future, keep an optimistic outlook, and develop resilience. The objective is to provide you with the self-assurance and knowledge required to accept this transition and transform obstacles into stepping stones on the way to your new job.

Seeking Guidance from ChatGPT During Career Changes: A Deep Dive

Taking the plunge into the world of professional change might feel like standing on the edge of a vast, undiscovered ocean. You're excited about the possibilities ahead, yet the immensity of the unknown might be intimidating. You'll use ChatGPT to lead you through this exciting but difficult voyage as your compass in this wide ocean. In this part, we'll go deeper into how AI can be your ally when it comes to studying new opportunities, sectors, and organizations, all while injecting a touch of professional charm to make the encounter entertaining.

Firstly, the magic of ChatGPT lies in asking the right questions. A question well framed is a problem half solved. When interacting with ChatGPT, specificity and context are your best friends. They can bring out the most accurate and relevant advice from this AI guide. Imagine you're an accountant with dreams of stepping into the vibrant world of marketing. You could kindle a conversation with ChatGPT like this:

"Highlight the key differences between a career in accounting and marketing"

"I'm keen to explore marketing. What skills and qualifications would I need to make a successful transition?"

"I have an accounting background. What marketing roles could best leverage my experience?"

By steering the conversation with such specific queries, you're tapping into the wisdom of ChatGPT to gain valuable insights that will illuminate your new career path, helping you to better comprehend the landscape and the ingredients for success. Using ChatGPT will also help optimize your time and efficiency as it will provide a direct answer to your prompts without you having to take on hours of tedious research.

Next, let's turn our gaze toward exploring industries. Each industry is a universe in itself, brimming with unique customs, challenges, and opportunities. Think of ChatGPT as your insider, a guide who can unveil the industry's mysteries. It can offer insights into the latest trends, growth projections, and potential stumbling blocks.

You might consider asking the following prompts:

"What are the emerging trends in the marketing industry?"

"How has the landscape of the marketing industry been reshaped by the rise of digital media?"

"As a marketing professional, what main challenges should I be prepared to face?"

You'll get a thorough grasp of the industry you want to pursue by utilizing ChatGPT's in-depth expertise, which will enable you to decide on your next career move in light of that knowledge.

Finally, let's not forget the importance of researching specific companies when contemplating a career change. ChatGPT can morph into your personal corporate investigator, helping you peel back the layers of company culture, values, and expectations. You could ask:

"What's the company culture like at XYZ Marketing Agency?"

"What core values does ABC Advertising Company uphold?"

"How do employees rate the work-life balance at LMN Digital Marketing Firm?"

By framing your queries in this way, ChatGPT can provide insights into the inner workings of potential employers, aiding your quest to find an organization that aligns with your career aspirations and personal values.

To summarize, ChatGPT is more than simply an AI tool; it is your professional advisor, filled with humor and wisdom and always ready to help you navigate the twists and turns of a career shift. You'll have access to an abundance of information by posing the proper questions and offering context, allowing you to make educated decisions about your future.

Identifying Transferable Skills and Leveraging Your Network

A cornerstone of any successful career transition lies in the ability to recognize and effectively present your transferable skills. ChatGPT stands ready to be your career counselor, helping you shine a light on the strengths and experiences you've accumulated in your prior roles that can be a valuable asset in your new career. Let's say you're a marketing manager eyeing a transition to product management. You could ask ChatGPT, *"Which of my skills from being a marketing manager would be applicable to a product management role?"* Acting as your personalized career strategist, the AI will sift through your professional history, helping you unearth key skills like project management, communication, and data analysis, which can be emphasized when you're pursuing a product management role.

A conversation with ChatGPT can also bring into focus how your existing skills align with the requirements of your prospective industry. For example, if you're a teacher aiming to rebrand your experience for a corporate training role, you could ask, *"ChatGPT, how can I reframe my teaching experience to suit a corporate training role?"* In response, ChatGPT might advise you to underline your adeptness at designing and delivering engaging content, your flexibility in adapting to diverse learning styles, and your proficiency at assessing performance metrics.

Furthermore, don't underestimate the power of your professional network during a career transition. ChatGPT can act as your networking coach, assisting you in identifying potential connections in your targeted field and providing tips on how to reach out to them for advice or opportunities. Suppose you wish to approach a former colleague now thriving in the tech industry for advice on making a similar move. You could ask, *"What's the best way to approach my former colleague for advice on transitioning into the tech industry?"* ChatGPT might suggest a sincere and considerate message like, **"Hi [Colleague's Name], I hope you're well! Your successful shift**

into the tech industry has been truly inspiring. I'd love the opportunity to learn more about your journey and any advice you could share as I'm contemplating a similar move. Would you be open to a chat?"

You can make new connections, grow your network, and open doors to your new career by creating unique messages and demonstrating genuine interest. Remember that your keys to effective networking are sincerity and sincere inquiry. In order to effectively communicate your intentions and demonstrate your passion for your new job path, ChatGPT is here to assist you.

To summarize, consider ChatGPT to be your lighthouse, helping you through the process of identifying transferable talents and using your network throughout a job move. ChatGPT will assist you in highlighting your abilities, making contacts, and finding work.

Handling the Emotional Aspects of Career Transitions

It's natural to feel a range of emotions as you traverse the unfamiliar waters of professional changes. Recognizing and dealing with these emotions is an important aspect of your journey. Having a secure place to express your views and worries may sometimes make all the difference. This is when ChatGPT comes into play. While it's crucial to note that ChatGPT is an AI and not a licensed therapist, it can provide a safe area for you to express yourself. It may offer coping tips, give useful information, and lend a sympathetic "ear" during this trying time.

Suppose you're grappling with a sense of being an imposter as you ponder diving into a new field. You could ask ChatGPT something like, *"How do I cope with imposter syndrome as I transition from accounting to marketing?"* In response, ChatGPT could share valuable tips like focusing on the skills you can transfer to your new role, seeking mentorship, or even practicing affirmations to boost your self-confidence.

If you're feeling a touch of anxiety about leaving the comfort of a stable job for an uncertain future, you might ask ChatGPT, *"What can I do to calm my nerves about this career change?"* ChatGPT might then guide you through strategies such as setting achievable expectations, breaking down your large goals into smaller, manageable tasks, or practicing relaxation techniques like deep breathing exercises or mindfulness meditation.

During those moments when you're in need of a little pep talk, you could turn to ChatGPT for uplifting quotes or narratives about individuals who've successfully navigated their own career changes. You might ask, *"Can you share some inspiring stories of successful career transitions?"* Your AI companion can offer you a dose of motivation, reminding you that you're not alone on this journey.

Should you be dealing with feelings of isolation or disconnect during your career shift, ChatGPT can assist you in brainstorming ways to build a supportive community. You might ask, *"How can I connect with others who are also transitioning into marketing?"* In response, ChatGPT could recommend actions like joining marketing-focused LinkedIn groups, participating in relevant Reddit threads, or attending local meetups to connect with others on a similar path.

However, it's important to note that, while ChatGPT can offer practical advice, if you're experiencing severe emotional distress, you should seek professional treatment. ChatGPT is intended to augment, not replace, the assistance and advice of certified mental health professionals.

In a nutshell, the emotional aspect of career changes demands equal consideration as the practical aspect. You may obtain useful insights and encouragement to manage your emotional journey through this big life shift by engaging with ChatGPT in a pleasant, professional, and even humorous manner. Accept ChatGPT's company, and you'll find yourself better ready to navigate the complexity of your professional shift with a renewed feeling of confidence and elegance.

We've discussed how ChatGPT may be a great ally during career changes throughout this chapter. ChatGPT can help you with anything from exploring new possibilities, finding transferrable talents, utilizing your network, and handling the emotional side of transition. You'll be able to successfully handle the twists and turns of your job transition and look forward to the exciting new chapter that awaits you if you use ChatGPT's guidance and assistance.

EIGHT

CLIMBING THE CORPORATE LADDER

~~~~~

Career progression isn't just about climbing the corporate ladder, it's more like a game of Chutes and Ladders—with some strategic moves, a bit of luck, and a few slides backwards now and then. As you navigate this game, having an AI as your co-player can make all the difference. In this chapter, we'll delve into how ChatGPT can help you make smart moves and avoid those pesky chutes. We'll explore how it can help you research companies, industries, and job roles, and provide guidance on how to assertively ask for promotions, raises, and increased responsibilities. But, wait, there's more! We'll also discuss the not-so-secret sauce to long-term success: balancing work and personal life. Because let's face it, even in a game, taking some time off to recharge is crucial. Ready to roll the dice? Let's go.

Researching Companies, Industries, and Job Roles

We've discussed how ChatGPT may be a great ally during career changes throughout this chapter. ChatGPT can help you with anything from exploring new possibilities, finding transferrable talents, utilizing your network, and handling the emotional side of transition. You'll be able to successfully handle the twists and turns of your job transition and look forward to the exciting new chapter that awaits you if you use ChatGPT's guidance and assistance.

Company Profiles

Think of preparing for a job interview or considering a job offer as embarking on a treasure hunt - the treasure being deep insights about the company that can give you a competitive edge. ChatGPT is here to be your personal treasure map, guiding you to uncover the golden nuggets of information about a company's past, present, and future.

The first stop on our treasure hunt is understanding a company's backstory. Just like every superhero has an origin story, every company has a history and mission that shaped its identity. To uncover these, you might ask ChatGPT something like, *"Spill the tea on Company X's origin story and mission"* The AI's response will provide a clear picture of the company's journey, its core purpose, and how it positions itself in the market.

Next, we navigate to the company's culture - the heart and soul of any organization. Getting a feel for the company's culture can give you insights into its work environment, values, and how employees interact with each other. Try asking ChatGPT, *"What's the office vibe at Company X? Are we talking suit and tie or hoodies and sneakers?"* This will help you gauge whether the company's work environment aligns with your own work style and expectations.

Now, onto the company's current scene and recent happenings. Staying updated about a company's latest news can give you a sense of its direction, challenges, and triumphs. This information is also handy for impressing interviewers with your knowledge about the company. To dig up this info, you could ask, *"What's the latest headline about Company Y?"* or *"Has Company Z made any waves in the industry recently?"*

The treasure you gather from this hunt - understanding a company's history, culture, and recent developments - will equip you with invaluable insights. These insights can not only help you assess if a company's ethos syncs with your own values and aspirations but also allow you to tailor your interview responses or decision-making accordingly. Remember, with ChatGPT by your side, you're not just a job hunter; you're a skilled career treasure hunter!

Industry Trends

Keeping up with industry trends is like surfing a wave—you want to be on top of it, not under it. Professionals must grasp the ebb and flow of their business, much as surfers must study the patterns of the ocean. Consider ChatGPT to be your surf coach; it can recognize waves and teach you how to ride them gracefully.

Firstly, ChatGPT can help you unravel the latest innovations that are causing ripples in your industry. Just as you'd ask a friend, "What's the hottest gossip in town?" you could ask ChatGPT, *"What are the buzz-worthy innovations in the tech scene?"* or *"What groundbreaking strides are being made in AI?"* This will keep you in the know about the latest tech toys and AI marvels that are reshaping the landscape.

Secondly, ChatGPT can provide insights into major shifts occurring in your industry. It's like having a seasoned industry insider who can explain the intricacies of market dynamics. For example, you could ask, *"How is AI stirring things up in the healthcare world?"* This will give you an overview of how AI is revolutionizing healthcare, from diagnosis to treatment and beyond.

Finally, with ChatGPT, you can gaze into the crystal ball and see the future trends of your industry. You could ask, *"What's the forecast for the renewable energy market?"* or *"What's expected to be the next big thing in the digital marketing sphere?"* This will equip you with foresight about where your industry is heading, allowing you to anticipate changes, prepare for them, and seize emerging opportunities.

Job Roles

As you ambitiously eye up the next rung on the corporate ladder, you may find yourself curious about different job roles that could be your next big leap. Think of ChatGPT as your personal career guidebook, ready to spill the beans about the ins and outs of various roles. It can lay out the day-to-day realities, the skills that are in high demand, and even the little-known peculiarities of different jobs. To get the 411, you could ask, *"What's the daily grind like for a marketing manager?"* or *"What tools should a data analyst have in their arsenal?"* or how about, *"How does the daily hustle of a product manager compare to a project manager?"* By probing ChatGPT in this way, you'll be able to get under the skin of various job roles and understand what skills you'll need to thrive, helping you craft a winning career development strategy.

Knowledge certainly is power in the game of careers, and ChatGPT is your hidden weapon. It may demystify the worlds of various firms, sectors, and job categories, providing you with the knowledge you need to make sound career decisions. You'll be well-prepared to negotiate the changing sands of the professional world and climb the corporate ladder if you engage with ChatGPT's advice. And the cherry on top? ChatGPT's comments can be seasoned with a dash of humor and a sprinkling of professionalism, ensuring that your research trip is not only educational but also fun.

Strategies for Asking for Promotions, Raises, and Increased Responsibilities

Asking for promotions, raises, or increased responsibilities can indeed be intimidating, but with ChatGPT by your side, you'll be well-equipped to make a persuasive case. The following strategies, supported by ChatGPT's insights, will help you present your case effectively while maintaining a professional yet personal tone.

Document your accomplishments: ChatGPT can assist you in creating a comprehensive list of your achievements, ensuring you don't overlook any significant milestones. For instance, you might ask ChatGPT, *"Help me list my major accomplishments in project management over the past year."* By demonstrating your value to the company with this detailed list, you'll have a strong foundation for justifying your request.

Research industry benchmarks: Knowledge is power, and ChatGPT can help you gather data on salary ranges and job responsibilities for similar positions within your industry. You could prompt ChatGPT with a request like, *"Provide me with salary data for a senior marketing manager in the tech industry."* Armed with this information, you'll be able to negotiate from a position of strength.

Prepare your pitch: Crafting a compelling narrative is key to successfully asking for promotions, raises, or increased responsibilities. ChatGPT can help you develop a persuasive pitch that showcases your contributions, highlights your potential, and clearly communicates your goals. For example, ask ChatGPT, *"Help me create a pitch for a promotion to a senior software engineer position, emphasizing my recent achievements and leadership skills."* With a well-prepared pitch, you'll be ready to make your case with confidence.

Choose the right time: Timing is crucial when broaching sensitive topics like promotions or raises. ChatGPT can provide guidance on when to approach your manager or supervisor, taking into account factors such as company performance, your recent achievements, and the broader economic landscape. For example, you might ask, *"When is the best time to ask for a promotion, considering my company's recent success and my role in a major project?"* By identifying the right moment, you'll increase your chances of a positive outcome.

Remember to have a professional yet personable tone throughout the process. Be sincere in discussing your goals and humble in appreciating your achievements. This approach will impress your boss, demonstrating that you are not just talented but also committed to the organization's success.

You'll be well-prepared to ask for promotions, increases, and greater responsibilities if you follow these techniques and use ChatGPT's observations.

Always keep in mind that ChatGPT is here to help you along the path, providing advice and inspiration at every turn.

Balancing Work and Personal Life for Long-Term Success

Achieving a healthy work-life balance is not only essential for your long-term career success but also for your personal well-being and overall satisfaction in life. In this part, we'll go through how ChatGPT may offer helpful advise and suggestions to help you strike the right balance while keeping a professional yet personable tone.

Time Management Strategies

Effective time management is crucial to maintaining a healthy work-life balance. ChatGPT can assist you in developing and implementing time management strategies tailored to your specific needs. Here are some additional prompts to explore:

"How can I create a daily schedule that balances work and personal life effectively?"

"What are some techniques for avoiding procrastination and staying focused during work hours?"

"How can I ensure that I have enough time for self-care and personal development while managing a demanding job?"

By exploring these questions with ChatGPT, you can receive personalized advice and strategies to optimize your time management, allowing you to perform at your best while preserving your personal life.

Stress Management Techniques

Managing stress effectively is essential for your mental and physical health. ChatGPT can provide a wealth of insights on various stress management techniques to help you maintain your well-being. Consider using these expanded prompts.

"What breathing exercises or meditation practices can I incorporate into my daily routine to manage stress?"

"How can I create a calming and stress-free work environment?"

"What are some strategies for managing work-related stress when it begins to impact my personal life or relationships?"

These questions will guide you towards specific stress management techniques tailored to your unique circumstances, fostering resilience and mental well-being.

Pursuing Personal Interests and Hobbies

To maintain a healthy work-life balance, it's vital to nurture your personal interests and hobbies. ChatGPT can offer guidance on how to pursue your passions while balancing work commitments. Try these expanded prompts:

"How can I find a local community or group that shares my interests in [specific hobby]?"

"What are some creative ways to incorporate my hobbies into my daily routine or work breaks?"

"How can I set realistic goals for personal development and growth in my hobbies while managing a busy work schedule?"

By engaging with ChatGPT on these topics, you'll discover new ways to integrate your interests into your life, enriching your personal experiences and fostering a healthy balance.

You may create a good work-life balance, which is essential for long-term success and happiness, by putting the techniques covered in this section into practice and making use of ChatGPT. You'll be better equipped to take advantage of opportunities, get through obstacles, and achieve long-term success in your professional endeavors with ChatGPT as your dependable ally—all while fostering your own personal development and well-being. Remember that a balanced life is a fulfilling one, and using AI tools can help you through every phase of your journey.

NINE

STEPPING INTO TOMORROW

~~~~~~

And just like that, we're at the finish line of our fascinating journey. We've traveled together through the pages of this book, exploring the potential of ChatGPT as a steadfast companion in your career journey. This AI marvel doesn't just hold the promise of being a tool; it's a paradigm-shifting powerhouse that can redefine your approach to professional growth, providing a wealth of insights, advice, and support at every twist and turn.

Throughout our shared journey, we've delved into the practical applications of ChatGPT, from unearthing your deepest passions to standing atop your career summit. We've experienced firsthand how ChatGPT can act as your personal career counselor in a myriad of ways.

Think of the times when you were preparing for an informational interview, and ChatGPT conjured up a suite of thought-provoking questions that made you stand out from the crowd. Or picture yourself at a networking event, and thanks to ChatGPT's guidance, you were able to craft engaging conversation ice-breakers that transformed brief encounters into meaningful connections.

Then there were those moments when you sought to turbocharge your skillset and become a more attractive candidate. ChatGPT was there too, guiding you towards online courses or certifications that perfectly suited your professional aspirations.

And who can forget the painstaking process of crafting persuasive resumes, cover letters, and LinkedIn profiles? ChatGPT made that process a little less daunting, offering expert advice that helped you tell your unique professional story in a compelling way.

And, when the big day finally arrived and you were preparing for an interview, ChatGPT was ready to help. It assisted you in generating potential questions and responses that highlighted your qualifications and fit, boosting your confidence and poise.

In each of these instances, ChatGPT proved to be a valuable ally, demonstrating its immense potential as a tool for career development and advancement.

Welcoming ChatGPT into your work path is like opening a treasure vault of resources. But it's more than that; it's a clear indication of your versatility and eagerness to ride the wave of technological innovation, both of which are very necessary in our dynamic and continuously changing professional world.

But remember, while ChatGPT is your friendly AI ally, it's crucial to strike a balance. Use it as a tool to enhance your decisions, not to make them for you. It's there to provide guidance and suggestions, but it should never replace your own instincts, critical judgment, and the invaluable advice of trusted mentors and professionals in your field. Technology should empower us, not make us overly reliant or remove the human element from our decisions.

As we tie up our in-depth exploration of ChatGPT's potential, I implore you to keep the flames of curiosity and open-mindedness alive. Embrace the opportunities that technology offers, and nurture an insatiable appetite for learning. The ever-changing employment market may appear to be a difficult mountain to scale, but with ChatGPT as your ally, you'll be well-equipped to negotiate the journey with confidence and agility.

As we come to a conclusion to our adventure, let me express my genuine thanks for your company. My sincere aim is that you've discovered vital insights and tools that will help you carve out a meaningful and successful career path, with new knowledge of using AI ad a useful tool. Remember that ChatGPT is right there with you, ready to support you in all your future pursuits, as you continue to unfold your professional potential.

So, let's stride forward towards a future aglow with promise and prosperity. A future where technology becomes our trusted ally, bolstering us to unlock our hidden potential, to scale greater heights, and to dance with our dreams. Here's to our shared odyssey in this bold, uncharted world, and to the boundless opportunities that await us just over the horizon.

Let's not just imagine this future, let's shape it together. Let's embrace the tools we have, like ChatGPT, to build bridges to our goals and ambitions. The journey may be long, and the path may be winding, but with perseverance, curiosity, and a little help from our AI companions, there's no limit to what we can achieve.

So let's toast to us—you, me, and AI. Here's to our shared appreciation of development and learning. Here's to tomorrow's exciting possibilities and the great adventure that lies ahead. Let's grab the now, embrace the future, and work together as a team to realize our professional goals!

TEN

RESOURCES, TIPS, & TRICKS

~~~~~~~

Now you're ready to make the most out of ChatGPT in your career journey. Excellent! This last section is designed to provide you with a comprehensive list of resources, tips, and tricks to help you get the most out of your interactions with this AI.

ChatGPT Resources

1. **OpenAI's User Guide**: This is your go-to resource for understanding the

technical aspects of using ChatGPT, including how to engage with the model, limitations, and safety measures. You can find it at: **https://www.openai.com/chatgpt**

2. **OpenAI's Community Forum**: An excellent platform to interact with other ChatGPT users, share experiences, and get answers to any questions you may have.

3. **OpenAI's Research Publications**: Want to understand the technology behind ChatGPT? Check out OpenAI's research papers at: **https://www.openai.com/research**

ChatGPT Tips & Tricks

1. **Be Specific**: ChatGPT works best when given specific prompts. For example, instead of asking "How can I improve my resume?", you might ask "What are some ways I can make my software engineering resume stand out?"

2. **Experiment with Prompts**: Feel free to experiment with different types of prompts to see what generates the best results. If you don't get the answer you're looking for on the first try, rephrase your question or provide more context.

3. **Understand its Limitations**: Remember that while ChatGPT is a powerful tool, it's not perfect. It doesn't have access to real-time data or personal experiences and is not a substitute for professional advice.

4. **Safety Measures**: OpenAI has implemented several safety measures to ensure that ChatGPT refuses outputs that involve illegal content, are hateful or offensive, or share sensitive personal information. Be aware of these while interacting with the model.

ChatGPT Prompts for Career Development

Here are some examples of how you may frame your prompts to get the most out of ChatGPT in your professional path to get you started. Remember, specificity is essential! Here are some additional prompts to consider:

Career Exploration

- "What are some emerging fields in the tech industry that I might consider for a career shift?"

- "Can you provide a comparison of the roles and responsibilities between a product manager and a project manager?"

- "What are some potential career paths for someone with a background in environmental science?"

- "What skills are needed for a career in data science?"

-

"Can you outline the typical career progression in the financial industry?"

- "What are some unconventional careers that could utilize my degree in psychology?"

Job Applications

- "Could you help me draft a cover letter for a software engineer position at a startup?"

- "How can I tailor my resume to fit a role in non-profit management?"

- "What are some unique skills or experiences I should highlight when applying for a job in the gaming industry?"

- "Could you assist me in crafting a compelling CV for a role in the fashion industry?"

- "How can I make my cover letter stand out for a position in digital media?"

- "What unique attributes should I emphasize when applying for a job in humanitarian work?"

Interview Preparation

- "What are some common interview questions for a role in data science, and how might I respond to them?"

- "Can you suggest some insightful questions I could ask an interviewer for a role in digital marketing?"

- "How can I best explain a career transition from finance to healthcare during a job interview?"

- "What are some behavioral interview questions I could face in a project management role, and how should I approach them?"

- "Can you suggest some probing questions I could pose to an interviewer for a role in the hospitality industry?"

"How do I effectively explain a career gap during a job interview?"

Networking

- "How can I craft a LinkedIn message to reconnect with a former colleague I haven't spoken to in a few years?"

- "What are some conversation starters I could use at a networking event for renewable energy professionals?"

- "How can I politely ask for a referral from a contact within a company I'm interested in?"

- "How can I introduce myself to a senior executive in my field at a conference?"

- "What are some good ice-breakers for a virtual networking event for sustainability professionals?"

- "How can I effectively request a mentorship from a professional I admire?"

Professional Development

- "What are some in-demand skills for UX designers that I could learn to enhance my career prospects?"

- "Can you suggest some reputable certifications for cybersecurity professionals?"

- "What are the key trends I should follow to stay updated in the field of artificial intelligence?"

- "What are some emerging skills in the field of digital marketing?"

- "Can you recommend some online courses for improving my programming skills?"

- "What are the most influential publications or blogs for a human resources professional to follow?"

Career Advancement

"What are some strategies for negotiating a higher salary at my current job?"

- "Can you give me some tips on how to ask for a promotion?"

- "What are some leadership qualities I should develop to become a successful team manager?"

- "What are some effective strategies for demonstrating my readiness for a leadership role?"

- "Can you provide tips on how to manage a team for the first time?"

- "How can I effectively communicate my ambition to move into a management role to my supervisor?"

Career Transition

- "How can I translate my experience in the hospitality industry to a career in customer success?"

- "What steps should I take to shift from a career in traditional marketing to digital marketing?"

- "How can I leverage my teaching skills for a corporate training role?"

- "What are some transferrable skills from the film industry to the marketing field?"

- "How can I make a career pivot from real estate to the tech industry?"

- "What should I consider when transitioning from a corporate job to freelancing?"

Personal Branding

- "Can you help me write a compelling 'About Me' section for my professional blog?"

- "What are some ways I can improve my personal brand on social media?"

"How can I present my freelance work in a portfolio effectively?"

- "Can you help me compose a powerful mission statement for my personal brand?"

- "How can I better showcase my creative works on Instagram?"

- "What are some tips for creating an engaging professional YouTube channel?"

Job Search Strategies

- "What are some effective ways to conduct a job search during an economic downturn?"

- "Can you suggest a strategy for finding remote work opportunities in the tech sector?"

- "How can I leverage LinkedIn for my job search?"

"How can I optimize my job search strategy in the field of data analytics?"

- "Can you suggest a plan for finding part-time roles in the event planning sector?"

- "What's the best way to use job boards for my job search in the automotive industry?"

Mental Well-being and Productivity

- "Can you suggest some techniques to manage stress during a job search?"

- "What are some time management strategies that could help me balance my work and personal life?"

- "How can I maintain motivation during a long job search?"

- "Can you suggest some mindfulness practices to help me stay focused at work?"

"What are some productivity hacks for managing multiple projects at once?"

- "How can I maintain a positive mindset during a challenging job hunt?"

Skill Development

- "What are some essential skills for a career in data science?"

- "How can I improve my public speaking skills?"

- "Can you suggest some resources to learn Python programming?"

- "What online courses would you recommend to enhance my project management skills?"

- "What are the most in-demand soft skills in today's job market?"

- "Can you suggest some books or resources to improve my leadership abilities?"

Remote Work and Digital Nomadism

- "What are some tips for staying productive while working remotely?"

- "How can I maintain a healthy work-life balance as a digital nomad?"

- "What are some of the best countries for digital nomads to live in and why?"

- "What tools and apps are useful for remote work?"

- "How can I avoid feeling isolated while working remotely?"

- "What are the best practices for leading a remote team effectively?"

Networking and Relationship Building

- "What are some strategies for networking effectively in a virtual conference?"

-

"How can I follow up with someone I met at a networking event without sounding pushy?"

- "What's a good strategy for asking someone to be my mentor?"

- "What are some tips for creating a memorable and impactful LinkedIn profile?"

- "How can I navigate a networking event where I don't know anyone?"

- "What's a thoughtful way to ask for a recommendation or reference?"

Entrepreneurship

- "What are the first steps to starting my own business?"

- "How can I validate my startup idea?"

- "What are some funding options for early-stage startups?"

"What key factors should I consider when choosing a location for my startup?"

- "Can you provide some tips for pitching my business idea to potential investors?"

- "How do I create a sustainable business model for my startup?"

Workplace Dynamics

- "How can I deal with a difficult coworker?"

- "What are some strategies for giving constructive feedback to my team members?"

- "How can I advocate for myself in a male-dominated industry?"

- "What strategies can help me manage work-related stress effectively?"

-

"How can I demonstrate leadership qualities even if I'm not in a management role?"

- "What are some tips for handling office politics?"

***

Keep in mind that these are merely beginning points. Feel free to modify these prompts to meet your individual requirements and career objectives. ChatGPT should be used in the same way that you would have a conversation. The more explicit and clear your queries are, the better your replies will be. Enjoy this great tool in your work toolbox, and best wishes for continuing success on your career path!

Notes: